RETIRE EARLY
WITH REAL ESTATE

A beginner guide to financial freedom

Eddy Moore

Retire early with Real Estate

Written by Eddy Moore

First Edition

Copyrights Notice

Limited Liability

Please note that content of this book is based on personal experience and various information sources.

Although the author has made every effort to present accurate, up-to-date, reliable and complete information in this book, they make no representations or warranties with respect to the accuracy or completeness of the content of this book and specifically disclaim any implied warranties of merchantability or fitness for a particular purpose.

Your particular circumstances may not be suited to the example illustrated in this book; in fact, they likely will not be. You should use the information in this book at your own risk.

All trademarks, service marks, product names and the characteristics of any names mentioned in this book are considered the property of their respective owners and are used only for reference. No endorsement is implied when we use one of these terms.

This book is only for personal use. Please note the information contained within this document is for educational and entertainment purposes only and no warranties of any kind are declared or implied. Readers acknowledge that the author is not engaging in the rendering of legal, financial or professional advice.

Please consult a licensed professional before attempting any techniques outlined in this book. Nothing in this book is intended to replace common sense or legal accounting, or professional advice and is meant only to inform. By reading this document, the reader agrees that under no circumstances is the author responsible for any losses, direct or indirect, which are incurred as a result of the use of information contained within this document, including, but not limited to, errors, omissions, or inaccuracies.

Table of Contents

Introduction

Financial freedom can mean a little something different for each person who is trying to achieve it. It is sometimes hard to imagine it because we often fall pretty to all of the advertisements and more that hound us from one day to the next.

Many of us are in a lot of debt and don't know how we are ever going to be able to get rid of it. But understanding why financial freedom is so important to us, and taking the steps to make it our priority can make a world of difference in how much success we can have with this goal.

There are actually quite a few benefits of reaching your own financial freedom, and as you start to get closer to achieving that goal, you will start to see how beneficial it can be to your overall goals and helping you to get some of the other things that you want out of life.

Real Estate urban legends

No money, no Real Estate business. Many people think they need to have money in the bank, high credit scores or connections to succeed in real estate investing. But it doesn't matter how much money you do or don't have right now. It doesn't even matter whether you own credit cards or how bad your credit scores are. You don't need to have any assets whatsoever, to get started in real estate.

You must learn the skills needed to be a good salesperson, and marketer. You also need the right skills to speak with investors and get their attention. Leveraging your sweat equity, time and knowledge can be a precious thing when done strategically. The better you get at helping investors see tremendous opportunity in working with you, the quicker you can turn your idea into a profit machine.

So, anyone can get started in it using different strategies to create income streams that turn the small idea into an empire. The top 1% of the wealthy on the planet all share this commonality. They all participate in real estate investing, and some started with nothing and built great careers and businesses thanks to real estate.

Banks are the only way to finance my real estate deals. Although this is usually the common route people take, banks aren't the only way to fund your deals. And if your credit score is as bad as mine used to be when I first got started, no bank will even consider loaning you any money.

Besides, banks cap you out anyways because they have so many restrictive rules and regulations even if your credit scores aren't too bad. Private investors are an excellent alternative and my number one recommendation. All you need to learn is the skill of raising private capital from individuals who are grateful that you can skillfully use their cash and credit in a way that brings them a profit (whatever their idea of profit is). If you can learn to create win-win scenarios and communicate this effectively to private investors, you can quickly and easily grow your real estate business.

Many people think that making money with real estate is quick and easy. If you're looking for shortcuts in life and lazy ways to make money where you don't add any value or put in the effort for the rewards desired, then I recommend staying away from real estate. Everyone will attempt to get you to buy into his or her program or product by over exaggerating the truth.

Real Estate investing requires patience, perseverance, and persistence. Believing false stories around real estate riches is setting yourself up for failure. The more knowledge you have, the better you get at execution and implementation, the higher your chances of success in the business. When starting out, you must be willing to invest a considerable portion of your time and effort to produce profit, especially with rental properties.

Becoming Debt Free

Imagine how it will feel. Imagine how your lie would change when there isn't any more debt! What would you be able to do if you no longer had to put your money towards credit cards, loans, mortgages, or any of the other debts that you have to deal with on a regular basis?

Instead of having to pay in all of this money to creditors for things that you purchased or used in the past, along with the interest that comes with it, you can take all of that extra money, which could be hundreds of dollars a month, into your cash reserves and investments.

While it may seem like in our very consumerist world that this is an impossible dream, if you work on it and are willing to give up some of the instant gratifications that come in our modern world, you will be able to make this a reality. It won't always be easy, but it won't take long for you to notice the good benefits that come with this endeavor.

Saving freely

When you aren't putting as much into your debts and paying off the creditors you have, you will find that it is easier to put more money into your savings. Many times it is hard to save. We either assume that we have no extra money to put into savings because we spend so much on little things that we don't need. Or we start to accumulate savings and then we see all of that extra money that is in the account, and we want to go and spend it on something big.

Your savings can be so important to your overall goal of financial freedom. While you don't have to add money to your savings and never touch all of it again, it is good to keep at least a little bit of money in your savings to help you out when things go wrong.

While we always hope and pray that the worst will never happen, things aren't always in our control. Having some savings for an emergency fund can make all of the difference in helping you to stay secure and not have to worry about your finances all of the time.

Some people wonder why they should put money into a savings account if you aren't able to get very much interest from it.

Since most savings accounts have such a low-interest rate on them, wouldn't it be better to invest the money instead? Savings is something that we naturally do when we start to spend less money than we have. If your income is exceeding your spending, you are going to have some cash around that you are able to use as you wish. You can save to build up a nice cash reserve, or to use to help you if a good investment opportunity comes your way.

Basically, it is always a good idea to have some sort of savings. You can use it or a good investment opportunity that comes your way. You can use it to help when emergencies happen. It is always a good idea to keep a bit of extra money to the side, whether it is in cash or in a savings account, for when the opportunity arises, this is true financial freedom.

Freedom to managing your Finances and avoiding stress

There is nothing that causes as much stress on you, both as an individual and as a couple, then your finances. Having to worry about the cost of things, whether you are going to have enough money to pay for the things that you and your family need, And when you and your spouse are both working hard in order to get things paid off, and there still doesn't seem to be enough to get through the month, it can be even more frustrating.

Stress about finances can be the worst and. You won't be able to get out of the debt without a miracle. It can cause a lot of fights between spouses because they are tired and worn out, and they are trying to find a way to make it better.

But think about how it would feel if you were able to avoid all of these problems and hassles? What if you weren't having to fight with your spouse each month in order to pay the bills and make things work out because you knew that you actually had enough in the account and saved up to handle it? What if you didn't have to worry so much, and you were actually able to do some of the things that you want, without having to sacrifice food and other things that you need each month.

Freedom of accumulating Wealth

When you work to reach the financial freedom that you need, you will find that wealth will be created. But you will only be able to create this wealth if you are able to create positive cash flow.

If more money is going out each month than you are making, or if you are breaking even, then how are you ever going to be able to build up wealth?

The nice thing with financial freedom is that you are able to step in and be able to put money into savings and use it the way that you would like. And the more that you are able to pay back, thanks to a higher income or less debt, the easier it is for you to build up the wealth that you want.

There are so many reasons why you would want to choose to gain your own financial freedom. No one likes to be in debt all of the time. They aren't interested in sending a ton of their hard-earned money to the creditors in order to pay off debts for things that they no longer use or appreciate.

We all want to be able to go on vacations, take days off when we want, and even retire early without having to worry all of the time. And this is where financial freedom and the steps that are listed in this guidebook will help you to reach these goals and see the results and the benefits that you want. In this sense, to become an investor you must first acquire the right mindset and probably change some habits.

Before starting to read this book, I suggest you to focus on the following points:

• **Save and invest** – Spend less than you make, invest correctly and save diligently. The amount that you need to save depends on the rate of return you will make and the time you have — upsizing your lifestyle when your income increases is a mistake.

When your income increases, you should increase the amount you allocate to savings. Have an emergency fund, so you don't have to use your savings. You should have a solid plan for how much you will save your paycheck. Try to invest your savings in an account that has a high-interest rate.

• **Start a business** – If you are offering services, you should create a duplicatable model. Outsource tasks so that you can focus on more important matters. If you're offering products, you need to determine how to manufacture, distribute and market your products profitably.

• **Create a solid financial plan** – Be prepared for as many situations as possible. What if you experience a financial setback? How and when will you invest? You don't need to imagine the worst all the time, but you have to know what to do if you encounter a setback.

• **Work with a financial adviser** – This professional can help you identify wise investments, create a plan and road map for your financial goals and determine areas where you can get higher ROI and reduce expenses.

• **Real estate investing** – Although you need to exert a lot of effort early on, everything will pay off eventually as you will be able to earn of residual rental income and enjoy the increasing value of your real estate properly. You're going to take significant risks, so be prepared for any ups and downs.

Chapter 1. Real Estate market

By now, you must be fairly familiar with the pattern of information shared in this book. The goal is to give you all the necessary tools required to make an informed decision. One of the most important of this information are the benefits you stand to gain from real estate and how it compares to other investment vehicles. You need to properly weigh the pros and cons and choose your preferred path to wealth.

Real Estate is a human necessity: basically, everyone needs a home to live, an office to work in or a warehouse to store goods, etc.

So, there are many types of real estate, from single family homes, to condos, townhomes, apartments, duplexes, co-ops, and much more. Real estate provides something that absolutely everyone needs. All these buildings are properties, which are built, sold, bought, rented, etc., in a continuous cycle called "Real Estate Market Cycle".

Real Estate Market Cycle

Without understanding market cycles, beginners are going into the market with mere assumptions and without right basic knowledge.

You may think that what works in Phoenix also works in Seattle, but it doesn't always work that way. Each market has different phases, and that is why you need to understand the market cycle. In simple and concise terms, here's what real estate market cycles are all about:

- The Recovery Phase
- The Expansion Phase
- The Hyper Supply Phase
- The Recession Phase

The Recovery Phase. Many new investors wonder why the phase of the market cycle begins from a recovery. What led to recovery? Well, a recession led to the recovery, but the recovery is like a rebirth. That's why it is usually considered as the first phase: a recovery follows a recession.

This phase is characterized by a slow but gradual growth for housing demand. You'll know it is a recovery phase when you begin to notice a gradual increase in the number of requests for building permits, a slight but steady rise in property showings, etc.

What's the use of knowing all of the above? Here's how to get the best from this phase: buy properties in leading locations in this phase before any rise in prices begins. You can also buy properties, fix them, and flip them in the next phase of the market cycle.

The Expansion Phase. Like an uptrend in a stock market chart, the expansion phase is where demand for properties is really high due to positive growth in the economy. There is usually equilibrium in the demand and supply of properties. The expansion phase is distinguished by fewer vacancies and a rise in rents. Confidently cash in on this phase to buy properties knowing that prices will continue to go up and rents will keep coming in.

The Hyper Supply Phase. When there is too much supply, the market has only one direction to go: downwards. This phase is characterized by a gradual increase in vacant properties and a significant drop in the cost of rent. During this phase, it is important that you focus on properties that have long-term value. Quickly identify owners who are willing to sell prime properties and buy them for the long haul.

The Recession Phase. For some reason, a lot of people do not recognize the signs of recession in the previous phase. Hyper supply quickly snowballs into a recession, which can be identified by very low demand yet high supply for properties, thus pushing vacant rates higher and dropping rental prices to an all-time low.

There are two ways to handle this phase: you either hang on and wait for the recovery phase, or take a risk and buy as many properties as you can. For most people, they wait for recovery. I'd advise you to take into consideration your experience and wealth stage before deciding to take on any high-risk investment.

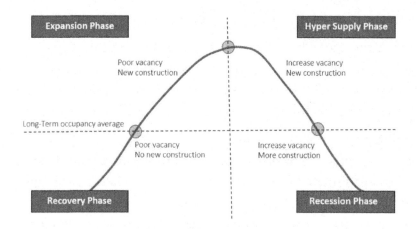

Real Estate Market Cycle

The Real Estate Market Cycle may seem complicated, but by looking at the market over time everything will become easier.

The Cycle can have phase variations and it is not mathematically certain that the phases occur in equal times: for example, the recovery phase can be a short and rapid transition to the expansion phase, or it can last several years. So, the cycles can have different durations and a general time different from previous ones.

Furthermore, the Cycle may vary according to geographical location and class of activity, so when applying the concept of a real estate cycle to a specific property, it is necessary to consider other possible factors. All this may seem complex and discouraged from engaging in this business but you must be patient and be well informed before proceeding. So, let's see what the pros and cons can be on the Real Estate business.

Advantages of investing in Real Estate

Here are some features that you might find favorable about real estate investments:

1. Steady Income: Making the journey to building wealth often comes with sacrifices. One of those is that you might have to forgo your day job in order to properly manage your portfolio. Rent and return on investment in trust funds can generate a steady stream of income for investors. To fully maximize this perk of real estate investment, it is important to choose properties that can generate sufficient income.

2. Financial security: Having a stable cash flow from real estate investments participates in the formation of a long-term financial security plan. Additionally, because real estate properties appreciate over time, your property is only going to become more valuable as time passes. This can give a strong sense of financial security indeed.

3. Inflation: Real estate investors do not get affected by inflation in the same way as other investors. In an inflationary economy, rental income and property value go up concomitantly. This often provides a hedge against inflation for real estate investors. Inflation is your friend because it can increase your cash flow and net worth.

4. Tax Benefits: Real estate investors get tax breaks on their rental properties. Additionally, the government often offers breaks for insurance, maintenance repairs, depreciation, travel expenses, property taxes, and even legal fees. The government does this because real estate investors occupy a special place in the economy as they drive the development of properties.

5. Self-employment: As a real estate investor with a steady income and a rapidly appreciating property, you are responsible for your own financial future. This means freedom from the routine of a nine-to-five job and having to listen to someone else tells you what to do. This is the most satisfactory advantage of real estate investment for most people.

Disadvantages of investing in Real Estate

1. High transaction costs: Compared to the relatively low transaction costs associated with purchasing stocks and bonds, real estate transaction fees are much higher. Sometimes, the transaction fees are high enough to discourage investors from investing in the properties.

2. Low liquidity: Investments in real estate properties have very low liquidity. Very often, it takes months to sell a property at market value. A rushed and premature sell-off usually comes with severe losses.

3. Active management: As mentioned earlier, real estate investments often require hands-on management. An easy way to navigate this disadvantage is to invest indirectly, in schemes like private equity funds. They take away the need for active management.

3. Liability: The legal liability is related with the use, sales, and trades of real estate. These assessments have become a necessary step for anyone who need to determine potential environmental liabilities associated with real estate transactions.

Chapter 2. Investing in real estate

Real estate investments like other forms of investments require extensive knowledge for success. You need to do some adequate research and check your facts properly before you commit any money into the investment. However, there are factors that can improve your success as a real estate investor: The Power of leverage and markets trends.

The power of leverage

Real estate has a major advantage that is stocks and other forms of investment: Leverage. Investing in a stock or a mutual fund requires you paying full price at the current market rates. However, leverage gives investors the ability to purchase more than they currently have the cash for.

Leverage can also be very risky. If market conditions change and the investment does not turn a profit, you will have to absorb the losses of the leverage as well. Use leveraging with caution.

Market trends

Market trends, above everything else, often determine how well a real estate investment performs. When the market is booming, prices climb at a favorable rate and investors often find it a good time to sell and turn profits. In downturns, market crashes and even recessions, for instance, savvy investors take advantage of the low prices of properties and buy as many as they can. They then flip them for a profit when the market recovers.

Market bubbles are a little more difficult to capitalize on. During market bubbles, prices skyrocket at astronomical rates and the public rushes in to buy. After a while, the bubble peaks and bursts. This often leads to crashes and may even lead to a mini-depression in severe cases. The best investors know how to profit from bubbles: Know when to get in; know when to get out; know when to stay out; know when to pick up the pieces.

By early retirement, I don't just mean spending the rest of your days lazily chilling on the beach sipping piña coladas (although you can do that too if that's your dream). Instead what I mean is being in a position to work on projects you love at your own schedule, eliminating the need for a 9-to-5 and spending more time with the people you love. Like Laptop Lifestyle, is the dream of everyone is desire to work few hours a week and still make a great living.

If that's your dream, if you've always wanted to find financial freedom and a stable, safe source of income real estate investing is the perfect tool to get you there.

Think of this book like a beginner crash course meant to help you fast track the learning curve, offer insights on pitfalls to be aware of and provide guidance on best practices. With that comes the need to know which path of real estate investing is going to be lucrative. After all, who wants to put in all the effort, energy, and resources needed if there isn't enough of a reward to balance things out? Well, I can assure you, an abundant harvest awaits you if you choose to plant the right seeds at the right time and tend to them as any good farmer in the field.

Real Estate versus stock or bonds

At the core of any investment is the income that can be generated. Real estate guarantees a healthy income stream for you if you know what you're doing. It's a dependable monthly income that you can rely on regardless of economic fluctuations.

Even if you own rentals that aren't doing so well, chances are you'll be making more reliable income than someone who has invested in other assets like stocks or bonds. That doesn't mean stock investment is a bad idea, it just means if you want something safe that is sure to appreciate over time, and if you don't like drama and the suspense of market flops, then real estate is the better option.

If you invest in a low-cost index fund of the entire stock market, you're probably going to create enormous wealth in the long run, but when first starting out, real estate is more advantageous in comparison to other passive investments.

For early retirees, it matters even more because real estate investing gets you steady income immediately whereas much of the game in stocks and bonds requires you never to touch it.

Real estate gives you more control over your money, how quickly you grow and the deals you invest in. Your skills and hustle become your best assets when you get into Real Estate investing. And if like so many people you lack cash for funding, your people skills become even more valuable. With a real estate deal, you can significantly improve a property and increase its rent and perceived value. And when you're also the one managing the properties well on the backend, that income stream remains under your control for years to come. Can you really control it?

Not quite. You can control when to buy, reinvent your dividends and when to sell it. End of story. The managers and employees of the companies you buy have more control over your success and income than you do.

There is no right or wrong in either of these options. But personally, it feels better when I know I can influence and control my investments.

Timing

It's another advantage when you invest in real estate. Real estate investing gives us something most passive index investments can't.

The ability to time my wealth building efforts. As someone with big dreams of financial freedom and early retirement, I'm guessing you've done your goal setting, and there's a due date you set for yourself. The only way to ensure your investments are growing and helping you reach that goal on time is by investing in the right things that are guaranteed to increase over a specific period. Preferably sooner rather than later.

With investments like stock indexes, growth can be extremely volatile over the short run. You always feel at the mercy of the stock prices, and if there should ever be a sudden dip or drop in stock prices, you can kiss your due date goodbye.

No chance of financial independence if the stock prices act up. This has been experienced a lot recently with Bitcoin and crypto-currency. It's a great game but a highly volatile one that's better suited for people who enjoy the drama and thrill of being in a never-ending roller coaster.

With real estate investing, however, you can breathe with ease because none of that drama and volatility applies. You have two very predictable growth options:

1) Positive rental income
2) Debt amortization (pay down)

Reliable rental income

Although I'm not here to make ridiculous claims that cannot be backed up (and we all know any type of investments does require risk management), as a general rule, real estate has shown it can remain quite stable even during the worst times.

Take for example the housing crisis that hit some years ago. On the surface, it appeared as though things were going really bad, right? However, research issued by the U.S Census Bureau on January 30,

2018, surveying current population and housing vacancy during the recession years as well as before that shows that even at the worst times in the market (2008-2010), rents still remained stable or only experienced a slight decrease in most U.S markets. Of course, everything else including housing prices themselves plummeted.

All this to state that although one is never wholly guaranteed that the investment will be completely secure in future as things change, suffice it so say investing in this industry is as close as you can get to a guaranteed win.

Amortization

Ever heard of a debt snowball? With a debt snowball plan, you can apply extra savings to pay off your mortgages faster than initially planned. Say twenty years earlier. In so doing, you reduce the risk involved and increase your income just in time to match that due date of early retirement.

These are predictable ways of determining when and how your wealth grows, and for the most part, you can easily control them.

Chapter 3. Early Retirement

Your retirement planning must be effective and should not take too long. Of course, it is important to start as soon as possible in order to increase your chances of having a higher interest rate more quickly than when you have to wait.

Also, there is the mindset problem. If you are not used to money you could spend more than you imagine or expect. On the contrary, if you put this money into your retirement project later on you will not regret it. So, when planning retirement, you need to have a longer-range vision, even though this may seem like a contradiction.

As you plan for retirement, don't just think about money. Also consider where you want to live, if you want to travel, what sort of medical costs you may have, and if you want to live luxuriously or more frugally. All of this will affect how much money you need.

Plan out your financial life after retirement, but don't forget about the non-financial situations as well. Who wouldn't like to have more free time? Friends, family, relax, etc.

Diversify your retirement savings

Do not put all of it into bonds or stocks alone. Always keep some in bonds, but do slant more towards stocks the younger you are.

Even within stocks, there are further options ranging from conservative dividend producing stocks to riskier but growth-oriented value stocks. If you are used to extravagant tastes, you may need to tone that down during your retirement. Your stream of income will be much smaller because you will not be working. Since less money is coming in, less should be spent. If you do not control your spending, you may run out of money in your retirement.

Enjoy yourself as much as you can when you retire. It's hard to know what to do with life as you age, but that is the reason you have to be certain to do something each day that aligns with your spirit. Find a hobby that you enjoy and stick to it.

Make sure your activity level does not decrease when you retire. It may seem enticing to spend time relaxing around the house, and this is o.k. sometimes, but it is important to maintain a reasonable fitness level. Walking is great exercise for seniors, but more demanding exercise should also be included regularly.

Safe money up for retirement

The best way to save up for retirement is to put money away starting when you are young. With compound interest the money increases based on what is in the account, so if you have $10 and add $1, the next year the interest will be based on $11 instead of $10.

To help ensure that your financial situation in retirement is sufficient to support the lifestyle you are certain to desire, it pays to consult with planning experts well in advance of your need. Taking the time while you are still working is a great way to make certain you have the sort of nest egg necessary to fund the things you value most.

Prepare yourself mentally for retirement, because the change can hit you really hard. Even if you are impatient to stop working, you may change your mind and become depressed. So, organize yourself with useful activities and start doing things right now that can give you a purpose in life. In other words, besides planning your retirement financially, he also plans your life, your interests and the things you love.

Don't forget to plan your life too, as you financially prepare for retirement. Most people learn early on that saving is very important, but they fail to take into account all the time they will have on their hands. Plan for hobbies, classes and volunteering, so you've got some productive things to do with your time!

Catch up on all of the credit cards that you have outstanding. This is important as it will reduce the amount of interest that you will pay over time, which you could be putting into a retirement account. Take care of the larger credit cards first and work your way down.

When you collect pension funds, remember the mortgage. For some people the mortgage is the largest account every month. You should try to repay it, so as to reduce your monthly debt, making your life easier with a fixed income. In an emergency you can also have substantial equity in your home.

Pension Plan

Does your company have a pension plan? Check your pension plan to understand more about how it is done and what benefits you will have. If you are considering switching to a new company, make sure you understand what that move will do to your pension benefit. It may not be worth it to make the switch.

Many people think they will have plenty of time to do everything they ever wanted to after they retire. As life progresses, the years shoot by faster and faster. Advance planning of daily activities is one way to organize your time.

Be careful when assuming how much Social Security you might get in retirement. The program will survive in some form, but you might see raised retirement ages and reduced benefits for higher earners. If at all possible, plan on saving up your entire retirement on your own, so that any Social Security funds are a bonus.

Never spend your retirement money. Pulling money from your retirement fund not only reduces the amount of money you have for retirement, but it also increases your tax burden. You will also be responsible for early withdrawal penalties, tax liabilities and lose interest from the amount withdrawn from your retirement fund.

You should know that once you reach 50-years-old, you can add extra contributions into your IRA to try to catch up. Before age 50, you are limited to contributing $5,500 each year. When you are over 50 that limit increases to $17,500. This is particularly helpful to those who started saving for retirement late.

Make sure that you look into your employer's retirement savings plan. Do some research, and figure out what sort of plans are available to you. Determine what sort of benefits there are for using the savings plan. Contribute what you can to it, and start saving for retirement as early as possible.

Social Security may not cover your living expenses. Social Security benefits only pay about 40 percent of the income your currently receive, and that will not cover the cost of your living. Most people need at least 70 percent of the pre-retirement income for a comfortable retirement, and that is 90 percent for those with low income.

Now it's time to check your expenses. How much do you spend on food, your home or car? These expenses won't go away when you retire, so you need to know exactly how much you will be spending once your income levels begin to drop.

Make sure your activity level does not decrease when you retire. It may seem enticing to spend time relaxing around the house, and this is o.k. sometimes, but it is important to maintain a reasonable fitness level. Walking is great exercise for seniors, but more demanding exercise should also be included regularly.

You should learn all about Medicare and how that plays into your health insurance. Understand the different implications of each plan. Having a better understand will help you understand the coverage you have.

Talk to a financial planner

A financial planner will help you determine how you can go about saving and spending your money without your principal income. You will be able to get a clear look at how much money you really have, and what kind of income you are going to need in the years to come.

Make a list of things you would like to accomplish. You don't need to call it a bucket list, but it is critical that you take the time to make a definite set of plans for your life after retirement. Having a purpose and a reason to get up each morning will make life more enjoyable.

Attend workshops that will give you some guidance on retirement. Employers and financial institutions often offer free seminars to people who are preparing to retire. You can get valuable information and advice from workshops like these. Take advantage of them if these types of classes are made available to you.

Training is important

Consider taking up a class or studying a foreign language in your retirement years, to keep your mind sharp. While relaxing is all well and good, the old saying "use it or lose it" applies in your golden years. Keep your mind active and focused, or you may risk becoming forgetful during the most fun years of living! When planning for retirement, create savings goals and stick to them. If you've already started saving, keep at it! If you haven't started, create small goals and make sure to meet them every month. Make saving a priority. Once you have met your goals, slowly increase them as you go along.

Do you want to maintain the same standard of living that you have now when you retire? So, you will need 80 percent, more or less, than your early retirement income. For this reason, it is necessary to start planning now.

You should save as much as you can for your retirement, but you should also learn how to invest that money wisely to maximize returns. Diversify your portfolio and make sure that you do not put all your eggs in one basket. When you spread your money around into different types, you will be taking less risk.

The belief is, once you retire, you'll have the free time to do all the things you've dreamed about your entire life. Time does have a way of slipping away faster as the years go by. You must plan well in advance for all of the typical daily activities you want to enjoy.

Some people seem to age more quickly after they retire. This may be due to inactivity, or perhaps just a loss of interest in life in general. It is important to focus on projects and activities that retirees are interested in. Retirement can be very enjoyable, but staying active is an important part of that enjoyment.

Have a plan for traveling during retirement, or you're probably going to regret it! Journey is a very enjoyable way of life but it is also very expensive, so having an adequate retirement plan can also afford to travel. Don't burn any bridges in your career as you face retirement, because situations can change quickly!

While it may feel good to tell your boss how you've really felt about him all these years, you may need to go back to work part-time and will want good references. Think first before you sign-off on opportunities.

Do the math and figure out how much money you need to live. If you ever hope to live without working, then you'll need to have that money saved ahead of time in your retirement plan. Figure out how much it costs you to live comfortably and this will give you some form of saving goal.

Take retirement seriously

Make sure you ask questions of the people that know what they are talking about. That might mean consulting with a financial adviser or sitting down with someone at your company to talk about what they offer. Keep meeting and talking until you have a handle on what you need to do to secure your future.

Make a budget for your current lifestyle and stick to it. If you are not able to live within your means now, your retirement suffers in two ways. You will never have a surplus of money to save up for retirement. You also would be unable to live within your boundaries in your retirement when your income is no more.

Think about keeping a part-time job after you officially retire, for a number of reasons. Primarily, it will help out a lot in terms of financing your lifestyle. Also, working is a great way to stay active and to keep your mind and body in great health as you get older.

If you don't know where to twitch saving for retirement, check with your employer. Many employers offer not only a 401k savings plan, but also contribute matching funds. Irrespective of how much of your income you should save, save at least the amount to get the full contest. Never leave free money on the table.

 Try to keep your retirement savings plan integral for as long as possible. If you drew on it to pay for an thrifty vacation for example, you risk losing a ton of money in interest and could even face penalties. While it would be nice to pamper yourself, you've got to think long-term financing when it comes to retirement!

Rebalance your entire retirement portfolio once a quarter. If you do it too often then you may be falling prey to an over-involvement in minor market swings. You can also end up putting money into huge winners. An investment adviser will be able to help you determine where to put your money.

Learn some interesting hobbies that you can continue when you retire. You will have a lot of time on your hands during your golden years. Hobbies and classes will keep your mind sharp and energy going. Something like art and photography are popular choices because they are not too physically demanding.

When trying to plan how much to save for retirement, you need to understand what your ideal retired annual income should be. Ideally, this should be around 2% of your total retirement portfolio, in order to make your portfolio substantial enough to last for your entire life expectancy.

Look into what type of health policies you may need. Health tends to get worse over time. As you get older, you can expect your medical costs to increase. Long-term health care plans mean that your physical needs are met even when things go bad.

Never spend your retirement money. Pulling money from your retirement fund not only reduces the amount of money you have for retirement, but it also increases your tax burden. You will also be responsible for early withdrawal penalties, tax liabilities and lose interest from the amount withdrawn from your retirement fund.

Saving money seems impossible, especially when you have little money left at the end of the day. Then you need to try cutting in other areas and putting those savings into your retirement plan. You will find that those few dollars make a big difference. Make certain that you have goals. Setting goals is good for many areas of your life, and it's really a good thing when you want to save money.

When you sit down and think about the amount of money that will be necessary later, then you will have better control over how to save it now. Try to have savings plans for the week, month and year.

Plan out your financial life after retirement, but don't forget about the non-financial situations as well.

If you haven't got as much saved up by 65 as you want, you can consider working part-time to compensate. You could also find a new job which is easier on you physically but keeps you going mentally. It might pay less, but you may find it more enjoyable.

Downsizing is great if you're retired but want to stretch your dollars. Even without a mortgage, there are expenses for keeping a large home like landscaping, electricity, etc. Consider moving to a smaller home, townhouse or condo. Doing so would help you save a considerable amount of money monthly.

Be sure to ask your employer about their pension plan. Though you may not think much about it when you are younger, this will become a big deal when you are older. If you are stuck with a shoddy pension plan, you may find it hard to pay your bills once you are retired.

If you are establishing a retirement savings strategy and you lack financial discipline, it is wise to never have the amount you want set back to ever be in your wallet.

You can set a specific percentage of your income to be regularly deposited into an account such as Roth IRA or 401 (k). In this way, the money will be automatically deducted from your salary and the choice will be enough if you want to save or spend the money out of your control.

Chapter 4. How to Think Like an Investor

In my early years of teaching real estate investing to new investors, I usually avoided over the mental phase of the investment and went straight into the heart of real estate.

I learnt that educating people on the techniques of real estate investments was actually very forthright. From the moment they had the information on the steps to take, the difference between success and failure was governed by what was going through their head.

Possessing all the information about investing will be of no use unless your head is clear. You will have to think like a real estate investor before being one. Your brain is a very powerful tool, but it's rather unfortunate it doesn't come with an instruction manual.

Your Why

Why comes before what. Why you choose to do something is of more importance than what you choose to do. Humans get easily excited about new endeavors. The moment the excitement wears off, however, we tend to move on to something else. The greatest achievements in life never happened overnight. In reality, it is usually the opposite.

The greatest victories probably took some time to achieve, correct? Investing in real estate is no different. At the point the excitement wears off and the newness of real estate fades away, what can give you a reason or reasons for venturing into the world of real estate investments?

The minute I started, I preferred to work from anywhere, be my boss, call the shots, make what I believe I deserved, make lots of money, and stay financially free. Was that too much to ask? On my job, I showed up at the office, wasn't free to work anywhere, I had no control whatsoever over my time, I took instructions from the boss, I wasn't earning what I deserved, I wasn't making lots of money, and I wasn't financially free. My earnings were my only salary and the only way that could improve was by hoping for a raise. These reasons were robust for me when I began. I refused to return to that life again and that motivated me to succeed.

Why do you pick to be a real estate investor? You are in the same situation as I was when I started? Maybe you are happy with your job and just have decided to invest your hard-earned savings in an investment with better returns than you are presently receiving.

You might be concerned that your cu Do you want more stint with your loved ones? Do you need more money? Do you desire freedom to see the world through traveling and exploring while you enjoy your life? Your why is your cause for becoming a real estate investor.

For your why to be operative, it must be very responsive. These sentiments drive our behavior. Binding this power enables us to achieve unexpected acts, far yonder what you believe is possible. rent financial status will not cover you properly after retirement.

The best part of finding your why is that the motivation you will ever need is already in you, instead of relying on others for motivation. Just discover what your why is in order to unlock an unlimited resource of power.

You are searching for what is absent in your life that should be present. This could be encouraging or destructive. You may be dreaming of living every day in a tropical ecstasy, calming in a hammock in the middle of two trees while cooling from a gentle island breeze. This thought creates significant motivation within you for creating that life you desire. What could be more significant to you right now is staying away from gratitude and raising funds for your children's college. Those feelings of pain from not being free from debt and not possessing the wealth to pay for your child's college education may weigh heavily on you. These negative emotions may act as a huge motivating factor too.

It is a fact, psychologists say, that negative emotions push us harder than positive ones. People will be more stirred to quit their jobs than to toil towards a goal of financial freedom. Turn this knowledge to your advantage first by thinking about every part of your life you never like which you believe hazarding into the world of real estate could solve. Your being very negative and emotional can be all the motivation you'll ever ask for in order to succeed in real estate.

Taking a moment, write down your why. A more emotional why gives you a greater outcome. Burn this need inside you every time you think about it. Your frustrations with how your retirement fund investments are performing along with the mere thought of how the lack of brilliance in your results gets you boiling mad, could do the trick. It could be that you are incapable to be with your loved ones almost as often as you would love to because of your present financial status. If nothing comes to mind now, spend time every day for the next couple of weeks thinking of it until you find it.

In the absence of a why, there are chances that you may not take the actions important to becoming a successful real estate tycoon. It's that vital. When someone is undeniably comfortable, they hardly have strong enough reasons to do somewhat different from what they are already doing. Knowing your hot buttons, what really makes you uncomfortable about your current scenario is the easiest and fastest way to having and maintaining dependable drive. Make this your first task for going into real estate investment.

Pain and Pleasure

There are two elementary inspiring factors in our lives, pain and pleasure. We decide to do something either for the desire it gives us or because of the pain we believe we could prevent by taking that action. For instance, your why may be the need to fulfill that drive of living your days on the beach with the sand and the sun.

This illustrates doing it for pleasure. Alternatively, your why could be that you don't want to remain in poverty anymore. That illustrates wanting to avoid pain. This concept is simple, we know, but this is exactly how the brain works.

Applying this simple yet very powerful ideology opens up a new world for you. You learn to motivate yourself in more than a thousand ways through pain or pleasure. For instance, some of the new entrepreneurs wrestle with the paralyzing effects of fear. They are afraid of talking to a self-driven seller, getting a contract signed, asking for nonrefundable urgent money from a buyer, and so on.

The complication here is that there are so many pieces of advice centering on thinking positive. Just thinking positive can sometimes push you to disdain fact in an attempt to exterminate fear. It's needless to turn a blind eye to the grim realities of life.

Fear could be a useful factor to us, on the contrary. Fear becomes a great counselor and an excellent guide.

Instead of eradicating fear, you could use it as a motivating factor.

Don't you think? Instead of worrying about, "what do I say to this homeowner," allow fear to inspire you into believing, "if I don't call this person, it could cost me $30,000 and that would absolutely overwhelm me plus I need that money." Preventing pain is a much stronger instigator than making efforts at gaining pleasure. People fight much harder to retrieve $20,000 someone stole from them than to save up in bits until it reaches $20,000 in their bank accounts. The drive to avoid pain is far greater than gaining pleasure. Arm yourself with this knowledge since it motivates you into taking action.

Specifically, when you get a moment in your investing journey, when fear starts to slow you down or paralyze you, start thinking immediately about the things you stand to lose if you do not take action. Think deeply about it until you begin to feel the pain which occurs when you refuse to take action. For instance, for some beginners, and sadly for some seasoned investors too, asking for nonrefundable, earnest money from buyers could be very terrifying and scary, even when it should never be. The irony is, the moment an investor gets burned once by a buyer who walks out from a deal and leaves the investor hanging, that investor would never be concerned about demanding nonrefundable earnest money.

There is a way to use the power of avoiding pain to push a new investor into getting nonrefundable earnest money from a potential buyer. They can hold this talk in their head, "If I don't demand non-refundable earnest money from this buyer, I will possibly allow this buyer to back out of the deal scot-free and that will cost me $37,000 as well as the time I have spent getting this deal to where it is, not to mention hurting the homeowner who is counting on me to help him". That is the way to use fear and pain as drivers to assist in taking the initiative. Instead of ignoring fear and pain, take charge of the emotions and allow them to turn your life around.

You're Comfort Zone

Do you know someone who knew unerringly what to do but simply refused to do it? Could that person have been you, maybe, sometimes? If that was so, could you explain why you fell into a trap of lethargy when you completely knew what you were meant to do? The answer lies somewhere in that space between your ears.

You interrelated pain to that major step so that although you knew how to do the task, you didn't do it just because your brain couldn't let you do it. Our brains work in such a way whereby both positive and negative feelings are linked to our thoughts. Labels of "pleasure" or "pain" are being persistently attached by your mind to each action you take.

For instance, property sellers are in the best position for many new real estate investors to talk to. Many new investors will take part in the following scenario, rather than speaking with the owner right away to understand the person's views.

They drive to the house, examine the outside of the home, look around and examine the neighborhood, go back home, and lastly, do all kind of online research about the property all before even communicating with the property owner.

The worst part is that the property owner's demands may be too high, or they may not even want to sell their property. All the time and energy invested as well as the travel expenses thus go to waste. Picking a phone to ask a few simple questions from the property owner would have fixed the problem instead of wasting time, energy, and money. This implies the person clearly prefers wasting time, energy, and money to making a simple phone call. People will do more than this to stay away from pain than to gain pleasure.

To buttress the example cited above, a phone conversation with the property owner is one thing that is out of the person's comfort zone. Driving around and doing online research were both well within their coziness. You have to repeatedly step out of your comfort zone if you want to keep being successful in life.

Your Comfort Zone and Your Money Zone Will Always be Equal. Comfort zone for each person is different. Perhaps, if the person could not drive a vehicle or was unable to navigate the internet, then a phone call would have been far comfier than the two.

If your comfort zone does not include the activities described in this book, then you would have to step out of your comfort zone. This may then include improving your communication skills over the phone, using computer to set up your business online, and so on.

You have to be ready to expanse yourself. Be always prepared to step out of your comfort zone. Why? That why comes here again. If you know your why, you should have the answer of the question of why stepping outside of your comfort zone is critical. Moving from activities that are not within your comfort zone to more activities outside your comfort zone is important for you to experience your biggest developments.

Attitude

Real estate investors who are ultimately successful have a unique attitude toward life. Such people do see every know-how as a test and every result as a learning lesson. This results in a state of mind that does not acknowledge failure. It never produces phrases like, "Well, that was a waste." An investor with the right attitude does not waste any idea. All experiences are tests, and all results are lessons.

However, pleasant and positive emotions are not always initiated by this attitude. At times, the lessons learned by successful investors are painful and despite all the pain, they do not turn a blind eye to the pain. They familiarize with it so that they do not have to learn the lesson again. Do not immediately believe a test is bad if you did not get the result you anticipated. This may be discouraging and not pleasant at the moment, but you may later realize that the lesson you learned was extremely worthy and essential for you to close the coming deal.

Successful investors are grateful to have the chance to invest. They have an insolence of thankfulness and show gratitude for the lessons they learned and the experiences they attained. When problems arise, they don't complain. They rather see them as experiments and view such situations as opportunities to learn.

Action over Analysis

The fear of the anonymous, the fear of making an error, and the fear of moving outside of their comfort zone do not allow many people to take action meanwhile the fear of not taking action at all should be their priority. We should know everyone makes mistakes when they first start a journey, and mind you, the more errors you commit, the faster you learn. So, your utmost fear should become inaction. In fact, for most successful investors, their only regret with regard to real estate business is not starting sooner.

Doing continuous analysis to the point of paralysis is a very common habit among new investors. Instead of taking action, they analyze and analyze until they are paralyzed. This arises from the fear of committing errors. Instead of taking up a deal or purchasing a property, they prefer reading several books and attending several seminars. They believe they must wait until they know much and have enough confidence to start investing. Meanwhile, in certainty, these expecting investors will never get to a level of knowing so much on real estate to be really poised until they take action. You tend to gain confidence when you take action rather than reading a book.

If you intend not to have only a short-term achievement in real estate, you must educate yourself regularly. Meanwhile, you must not just educate yourself; you must be taking actions too. Investors must learn new techniques and new ways of investing. In real estate, a point of total understanding of all the aspects cannot be attained. Therefore, waiting to have total confidence before taking a step will paralyze the person forever. An action is far more powerful than analysis. This is exemplified when an investor who is not afraid to try new things but with less knowledge gives a far better and faster result compared to an investor with less action and much more knowledge.

Commitment

Success is always a result of long-term dedication. All successful real estate investors in the world have one thing in common that they stick with their job until they accomplish it.

You must be ready to make an intense and requisite assurance to stick with it until you succeed so as to make sure you attain your goals. You should try to always have positive thoughts which will help you succeed in life. You should be determined not to quit real estate work until you succeed. The key word in that sentence is, "until." That's what is called commitment.

In a world of starters, you will want to be a finisher. Do re-examine after attaining success in your effort. This is how successful people think. They tell themselves, "I will continue to do this until I succeed", then I can re-examine.

If you want to become a successful real estate investor, make a commitment right here, right now, and stick to it until you are successful. Fortunately, you are on the road to greatness if you can make this commitment to yourself, your family, and your future.

After reading this book, you can start putting this new commitment into use.

Possibility Thinking

Successful investors know a deal won't work due to many reasons, and when they detect at least one reason why the deal will work, the real big money is made. This is called possibility thinking. Do not stand on why things won't work, rather think of how it can work. Instead of thinking positive, which can neglect reality and literally stop growth, possibility thinking includes exploring the cold, hard facts of a situation and thinking of creative ways to sort it out. Here's a quick way for your possibility thinking muscle to be developed. When discussing or making a decision with another person next time, avoid using the word "no," and instead, replace with, "yes, but." This will make you start thinking deftly, and you will be able to come up with other ways to solve problems. You must always think in terms of possibilities if you want to be a successful real estate investor.

Any transient roadblock one may encounter in real estate investment will be much like the fence. It can be overcome because the ability to overcome it is in you. A simple four-foot fence cannot stop you from liberation. You should know that.

Repetition

For you to be good at something, you must do it over and over again... Even if you learn quickly, or you retain new information easily, repetition is still the key to mastery.

Reading the same information over and over again can be noticeably enlightening. In addition, as your view transforms, you will see concepts and ideas that you never noticed before.

After reading this book, apply the skills and methods you learned repeatedly. At the end, they will get rooted into your subliminal and you will be able to apply them automatically without even thinking about them because they will already be in your sub-conscious mind. When you can literally do real estate investing while asleep is when it becomes easy. The most successful investors have automated their minds to think like investors. That comes with repetition.

Humility

An investor must be humble. History made it known that there are many eminent people who have failed due to pride and overconfidence. Doing more listening than talking and being insightful, removing one's ego, and endeavoring not to make assumptions are attributes of a humble person. A humble person doesn't get angry easily or get troubled. This means one has hugged changes, allow challenges, and come to know that everything cannot work out as intended.

You be likely to learn from your mistakes and open your mind to new ideas when you are self-effacing. People who think they already know everything have difficulty in embracing new ideas. Some call this behavior as having a full prize. Those with full cups fail miserably in real estate. When your cup is empty, you embrace new ideas and success is yours.

When you put blame on yourself for your shortcomings in business instead of putting it on others, it is called being humble. When you take responsibility for your successes and failures and have the mind of learning from them, you will become a successful investor.

Humility is an indication of strength and not weakness. You can be humble and yet still be a self-assured and bold leader. However, there is a thin line between superiority and composure, between being full of oneself and being sure of oneself. Successful investors are humble and self-assured.

Taking Advice

Advice can be a very useful thing. Each person has an opinion. But to know who is right, the person who has already made intense results in a given field is usually the person that's regularly right.

The first few months are a very important and fragile time for beginners of real estate investment in their development. It is at this point that many good-intentioned family members, friends, and associates give their opinions. Beginners must not listen to the destructive voice in their life. It may cause them to leave or pull back from giving it their full energy.

To prevent the worse from happening, always seek your advice on a subject from a trustworthy source. If the person giving an advice on real estate has gained a complete fortune, you can listen to them. If not, do not ask for advice from such a person. Make sure the person who you want to follow the guidance from is a duplication of somebody you want to turn out to be.

At times, people who tend to counsel new financiers on real estate business are those who have failed wretchedly at it. It may be a friend who has invested in it in the past and did not make anything from it. It may be a family member. Do not make the mistake of listening to them. The best people to get advice from are those who know about the business very well and very successful at it.

For instance, parents are regarded as a great choice for seeking advice on how to raise children. But if such parents were financially incapacitated throughout their lives, it will not be advisable taking advice from them on how to be financially capable because they have not experienced such a thing. We follow our parents' advice on things because that's how we were raised, even though they are not the most qualified to give us the advice in many fields, be it our career or finances. Most of us usually have that person we confide in for giving us good advice on things but do we think whether that person has what it takes investment-wise? We should be careful of taking advice from people that are financially incapacitated. Not taking their advice does not mean you are rude; you are just being careful and realistic.

Thus, ensure that those advising you on real estate investment are worthy of it. Make sure the person advising you is an expert in the field. If not, do not take the advice. Most times, people who are not experts give you bad advice. However, if a lawyer who is an expert in real estate investment advises you on the business, do not hesitate to take his advice because he definitely has the experience.

After making sure the person advising you is an expert, you need to know the reason why you are being given that advice. You should be able to know the perspective from which the person is advising you so as to know if it will help you in your endeavor or not. Take, for instance, the example of the real estate lawyer.

Maybe at the time the lawyer is advising you, a new law is about to be enacted that affects the way he could advise his clients, so he will be hesitant in providing you the information you need. Another example may be an agent that tries to discourage you from buying a property because he wants to buy it himself, but just waiting for you to leave the idea of buying it.

The issue is similar to asking a barber whether you should get a haircut or not. Normally, the barber gets paid for the haircut, so you should expect he will answer in his favor, which means he will say "yes, you do need one" because he will be profiting from it.

That brings us to how to overcome getting bad advice from people that are expert in the field. The best solution is to make sure your interests go along with their interests. For example, if your lawyer knows that he will be getting paid as you close each real estate deal, he will make sure he does everything within his means to make it successful, by giving you good advice. Or, if you compensate your real estate agent on every property, he helps you in buying or reselling, he will make sure he does his best. People that are successful in real estate business make sure they align everybody's interest because, in the real world, people work very well when they know they have something to gain.

This is how our apprentice program was built, on mutually aligned interests. The profits are shared with us by our students 50/50.

When they win, we also win. This gears our interest in giving them the best advice because our interests go hand in hand. When the student makes money, the gurus also make money.

We shall talk about the elephant in the room. You maybe believe by now that I am the ultimate source for advice on real estate investment. But how will you know the advice I am dishing out is best for you?

Right techniques and strategies should be used by students to close deals; money is made when the students close a deal.

Who is Your Mentor?

There is no successful person without a mentor. We must know there is no self-made successful person. Every efficacious person has an advisor, or mentors, that have taught and trained the person. The natural effect of this is that it's the fastest shortcut to success. Having a mentor helps to speed up your success.

You must have a mentor

When choosing your mentor, choose wisely. Mostly the first person new investors meet is the one they tend to align with.

Meanwhile, not having a mentor in real estate is the worst thing ever. Fortunately, figuring out the value of a mentor is not difficult.

When taking counsel, you will want to make orthodox yourself with people who are more successful and know better than you do about a subject as I have previously said. You should be able to determine the quality of a mentor by what they have personally achieved in real estate and also through the people they have mentored in the past. Do not allow someone who has never mentored anyone in the past to be your mentor even if they are greatly rich in their own right because mentoring is a skill unto itself. Be someone's mentee who is in good books for mentoring others into success. There is no time to be someone else's mentee guinea pig. Choose a mentor sooner rather than later.

Partners. Most investors take the usual step of adding on a partner to their inexperienced hustle when they first get started.

Mostly new investors want a partner because they do not want to invest alone, thinking their partner will bring a great value or the person is important to the job. Partnership is useful in business only if it is organized, and you partnered with the right person.

First of all, you should partner with someone for a definite period of time. It's common when two friends partner up in business, the timeframe for their partnership is not always detailed and later when the unescapable occurs, they will want the business to head in different directions. Unfortunately, they end up not going along well, and the business wavers. The best way to avoid this is that the partnership should have a timeframe from the onset.

Secondly, the partnership should be with someone providing a great value. A clash can occur in partnership when it's only one partner that's doing all the work or providing all the value, and the other partner is indolent and useless. To avoid this, ensure each partner brings value above and beyond just working in the business.

In addition, the role as well as the responsibilities of each partner should be made known to them.

In a business partnership, one must be ready to think about what's going to end the business although they may feel uneasy about it.

Ensure your partner is providing great value if you have already engaged yourself in a partnership. Put up a timeframe for the partnership to end, and draw a plan for who is going to be accountable or responsible for whatever happens. If your partner is not in line with this, then you are likely to have an unsuitable partner.

Understanding the fundamentals

Good real estate investors do not strive to get rich quick. They are not interested in overnight success. Thriving real estate investors enter the game fully informed and aware of the dedication, perseverance, and hard work and self-learning they'll need to take on, and they are willing to go all in.

Are you?

If your answer is absolutely yes - then it's time to step up.

The game is about to begin, and we need to be fully prepped for what is ahead. That means, understanding the basics. There are some concepts to be known before starting the business of real estate investments. Failure to understand these concepts means you will encounter more overwhelm, confusion and roadblocks than is necessary.

Ever been to a doctor's office to get treatment only to come out feeling a bit confused because nothing he said made sense, but you paid a hefty fee anyway and trusted that he knows what he's doing?

It happens to me a lot. Sometimes I come out with a list of medication, take them to the pharmacy and trust that between the words on the paper and the knowledge of the pharmacist, I will receive the right medication prescribed to me which by the way I can't even pronounce. There's a lot of blind faith involved in such situations (for many of us).

Real estate investing should not be like that for you. If you don't speak and understand the "real estate language" you won't go very far. It is your job to self-educate and master the language.

Chapter 5. Traditional Vs. Innovative Investing

Traditional real estate has been the same for the last 100 years or so with very minimum shifts. People usually buy and sell houses using real estate agents as the gatekeeper. In the United States, about ninety percent of transactions involve an agent while the remaining ten percent do private sales. In the U.K agents take up more than ninety percent of the share.

In the old days, this was probably the only business model to follow if you wanted to be part of the real estate game and much of it still continues to take place offline even with the introduction of technology. However, something is starting to shift.

New models are now launching all over the world and investment in the industry is growing. We are now starting to see the emergence of real estate tech companies and innovative entrepreneurs coming out of the woodworks with disruptive concepts that help empower their clients and get the job done.

We are also seeing more creativity in how transactions are carried out. Perhaps there was a time when you had to be wealthy and have high credit scores to be a real estate investor. That's why people started believing that as the only viable option of entering this business. But as I proved to you in an earlier chapter, this is definitely not the case today. Your possibilities are now endless, and as long as you have the hustle and a good plan, your chances of success are very high with or without capital funding.

Creating your real estate business plan

Creating your business plan is one of the first steps toward long-term success. As any architect will tell you, constructing a beautiful building that lasts over time is impossible without proper planning. This is you ensuring the foundation is solid before breaking ground.

What a business plan is not:

This isn't meant to be rigid rules that constrict you. It's supposed to be a roadmap or a guide that helps you move in the right direction. It gives you a measurable, logical reference point to keep yourself accountable.

With a clearly defined business, you're supposed to feel more motivated, able to envision the end game and carry out the plan from your current starting point.

Here is what your real estate business plan needs to include:

Goals

What objectives matter to you? What would you like to achieve? If you desire to make $10,000 a month from your real estate business, write it down. If your goal is to own 20 units in the next 2 years, write that down.

Goals may change over time, and that's okay. As you hit an objective, you'll set a new one and restructure your business. That's how it should be. I recommend setting short-term goals and long-term goals. Make sure these are goals that fire you up and align with your overall vision of your life.

Mission Statement

We've heard from motivational gurus the importance of knowing your "WHY." It's not hype; you do need to know what's driving you to make real estate investing work for you. And it needs to be something deep and meaningful to you so that when things aren't going according to plan (and it always happens), you'll have an anchor to keep you going.

Your mission statement needs to define your purpose, the purpose of your business and how you're going to benefit your clients.

The strategy

As you're about to find out, there are hundreds of ways for you to make money in real estate. That's a good thing. However, you must be careful not to get sidetracked trying to implement all of them at once. In fact, I share the most relevant ones to you in the hopes that you will take just one of these strategies and master it.

You don't need to be a master at everything in real estate to make good money. Think of this is choosing a vehicle. You only need one vehicle to move from point A to point B. Your point B is the selected goal. That is your desired destination. Now you simply need to choose the vehicle you'll travel in and stay focused on the journey till you reach the destination.

Writing down the strategy of your choice helps to anchor it in. It also gives you the chance to evaluate how well it aligns with your mission, your goals, your current situation and the empire you're building. I've already alluded to the fact that there are many niches and strategies in real estate investing that work regardless of your financial situation.

If you're going to work part time or full time on this, you'll also need to pick the appropriate niche and strategy that has the potential of generating the highest return on your investment. Don't worry if you're still unsure which is best for you, come back and fill out this section after going through the next chapter.

Realize also that you can always expand and take advantage of more strategies as you grow and scale the business.

Timeline

Setting smart goals also included giving them an expiration date. You need to pick the desired time that feels realistic but at the same time stretches you. A 23-year-old girl aspiring to be a real estate investor said to me that her goal was to become a millionaire and move to New York by the time she was 25 years old.

She gave herself 2 years to go from a complete newbie with no money in the bank, lots of student loans and no mentorship to being a millionaire investor. While it does sound sweet and ambitious, she's setting herself up for failure.

I want you to avoid making yourself the bad guy in the story of your life. Pick a due date for the goals you've just set and do it intelligently knowing that whatever choice you've made, you'll have to be accountable to yourself when the time comes.

The Market

As a beginner, you need to choose an area that you will dominate and the type of properties you'll look for first. You're a new investor with little or no experience so you need to plan on investing in a property that you can easily access. Your local area is often the best and most comfortable place to start because you know the area, feel comfortable enough to live there as well, and it's easy to drive to the property. Of course, there are some exceptions to this in which case you can invest in other areas, but I do recommend starting locally. Identify the local players, start creating allies, learn as much as you can about the properties and opportunities in your local market and you'll find it's easier to become a local superhero.

When people trust you, it's easier to do business with you.

Criteria

The next thing we want to make sure you write down in the business plan is a strict criterion of the deals you'll start working on. What kind of deals do you wish to work with? What criterion should each property possess? You also need to define your loan to value, cash flow requirements (critical), the maximum purchase price, the maximum rehabilitation budget, and the maximum timeline.

One of my first mentors taught me years ago that having a strict criterion and adhering to it no matter what would save me a lot of heartaches. And he was right.

If a deal doesn't meet your criteria, walk away. Most people won't because they either haven't created a set of rules for themselves or because they get seduced into a deal blindly. Either way, those people usually end up with heart-wrenching stories of deals gone back. I'm not saying you can't land on a bad deal, but at least by having a clearly defined criterion, you can easily recognize properties that won't end up being a good deal, at least ninety-nine percent of the time.

The Marketing Plan

In today's world where people spend most of the time online, it's never been more critical to craft a marketing plan that serves you both offline and online. You can't just depend on traditional marketing methods.

There is great power in technology, and if you're not coming up with creative ways to show up on your clients' mobile phones, you'll not be able to survive and grow in an on-demand environment.

So, you need to have a marketing plan that helps you reach buyers and sellers effectively. Start thinking of how you can generate constant leads of motivated sellers. Ways for finding the best deals that are listed. Will you use agents, MLS, direct mail to lists, online searches, paid ads or other means?

The Financing

This is usually a very challenging part for many beginners. Today's market requires you get innovative and resourceful especially if you don't have the cash to start with. Write down how you plan to acquire and fund your deals. Will you be using conventional means? Will you get equity partners, seller financing, lease options, hard money lenders or some other innovative method?

There are simple things you can learn to become more attractive to private money lenders which is good because that ensures you always have a steady flow of financing whenever a deal presents itself. We'll cover this more in the chapter on financing your real estate investing.

Your current finances are also essential to include in the business plan. What resources do you have? Are you starting with zero or some equity and cash? Document this and update it as it changes.

Documenting the steps for closing the deals

Carefully write down the steps you are going to use to turn a property purchase into a profit. Include the income and expenses and prepare for the unexpected as well. Detail some of the exit strategies that you know can work in case the plan doesn't go as expected.

Exit strategies

You always need a backup plan for your original plan, and then you need a backup for the backup. I kid you not. Having multiple exit strategies is essential especially in the beginning because without it, you might end up stuck with a property that has no cash flow and that would be hell!

So, this part should take up a significant portion of your business plan. How are you going to get out of the deal if you need to? Write down as many back up ideas as you've got.

This is where mentorship becomes super useful. Books, seminars, and courses are great, but having a mentor who can share different tricks and perspectives is priceless. That's the stuff you'll never get in a book because it only happens during that live human interaction.

A few exist ideas to get you started are, you could flip the property or sell the note or rent and hold. We'll talk more about this in the chapter on the exit strategies.

Building the vision

This is one of my favorite parts when going through this process. It's where you get to paint a detailed picture of the next 10 years and where you and your empire will be. Start in a new page in your business plan document and vividly describe what your business will look like in an ideal (but practical) way. Allow your imagination to take over and show you what's possible. Detail the purchases, cash flow, appreciation, trades, 1031 exchanges, cash-on-cash return and more. Make sure the goals you set, the mission statement and this vision align. You may not know how to get to the vision and chances are the path will not be straightforward but putting it down with as much clarity as possible is the first step toward making it a reality.

One last thing to remember here is that it doesn't have to be perfect and you shouldn't expect the journey to go exactly as planned on paper. It is good to have this detailed document, but you're bound to hit some obstacles along the way and experience some failure. As long as you remain flexible and focused on the long-term vision you defined for yourself, success will be inevitable.

Many investors who've experienced great failure attribute a considerable portion of it to lack of preparation and proper planning. Now you know how to avoid falling into the same trap.

How to invest with little or no money

I am super passionate about this part right here. Coming up with creative ways to run successful deals that turn a profit with no money to is what changed my life when I started out. I want to give you the nitty gritty on how you can invest in real estate without cash or credit. If you want to make things happen, you'll need a couple of things.

First, you'll need to find the right deal. I have a whole section devoted to this so you'll find helpful tips on how to do this right if you're feeling overwhelmed. Just know, there is a surplus of deals right where you are and with the right mindset and a lot of research you can find one that sets you on the highway to success.

Second, you need to have the right knowledge because if you're not knowledgeable in real estate, you won't get very far. There is no cheating in this industry, those with more knowledge and people skills always come out as winners no matter what anyone else tells you. For those starting out low on cash, this part becomes even more critical as it can become the one thing that gives you an edge and causes an investor to go all in on you and your deals. Do whatever it takes to acquire the right knowledge and continue to learn as much as you can about this industry.

Third, you need to create a way of funding the deals by bringing in someone who can bring in the money. Because when dealing with real estate investing, it does take money. It always takes money; anyone who tells you different is only revealing their lack of expertise in this industry. But it doesn't have to be your money.

The best way I've found to make a lot of money when starting from scratch is to either do a lease option or build a relationship with a partner (with a 50-50 agreement) where they bring in the credit and cash, and you run the deals, bring the knowledge, organize a solid team, etc.

By leveraging your skills and ability to get awesome deals in play, any good partner with money who wants to become wealthy as well should be more than happy to form a partnership with you.

A big Real Estate investor pays a great testament to how brilliant this strategy of forming partnerships can be and in fact, said that he made his first million dollars with less than ten thousand dollars of his own cash.

Chapter 6. The best type of Real Estate strategies

These are the most common strategies to make money with real estate. I have focused mostly on strategies that any new investor can leverage regardless of their financial situation. Bear in mind that in this section our emphasis will be on profitable strategies that are time tested and proven to work even for people with no prior experience.

House Flipping

Flipping houses has become a very popular practice. Perhaps it has something to do with the numerous cable television shows promoting it. Regardless of why it's becoming so popular, house flipping is a strategy I recommend testing out if it resonates with you.

It involves buying a piece of real estate at a discounted price, adding value by improving it in some way and then selling it for a profit. A similar model to help you envision this is the standard retail model of "buy low, sell high."

Since the single-family home tends to be the easiest to buy in real estate, it's the most popular type of property to use this strategy on.

For example. A home is worth $250,000 if it was in perfect conditions, but it needs $35,000 worth of rehabilitation work.

An experienced house flipper would be able to purchase this home for $175,000 ($250,000 X 70% - $35,000) and seek to sell it for the full $250,000 once the rehabilitation work is completed.

Please note this is merely a rule of thumb and actual numbers verified and adjusted to ensure a profitable and successful flip.

Avoid this mistake: Don't make the mistake of assuming this is a passive income strategy. House flipping requires effort and active, hands-on participation as well as speed and efficiency if you want to make money from it. In essence, it is like having a job because you only make money when you flip a house.

Speed is essential when it comes to house flipping. You need to buy, rehabilitate and sell the property as fast as possible to ensure maximum profit and to avoid many months of expensive costs like property taxes, utilities, financing charges, condo fees (where applicable) and any other maintenance bills required to keep the house in good physical or financial standing.

Wholesaling

This is a strategy few people know about, and even fewer teach it well. And when done right it can literally launch you into your first million with no cash down.

Technically speaking, wholesaling is a process that requires you to run a deal without ever owning the piece of property you're attempting to sell. Sounds confusing right? Let me see if I can simplify it more.

The wholesaling process involves finding really great deals, writing a contract to acquire the deal and selling the contract to another buyer and receiving what we call an assignment fee. This fee typically ranges between $500 - $5,000 and higher depending on the size of the deal. In other words, it's about being a middleman who gets paid for finding great deals.

A wholesaler is really great at marketing and finding incredible deals. As a wholesaler, you can sell your contracts to retail buyers or to other investors such as house flippers who are usually cash buyers.

This strategy requires someone with strong people skills and someone who is willing to go the extra mile to build solid relationships and credibility within the real estate community. And because most of the buyers are cash buyers, you'll often get paid within days or weeks.

It is most definitely a low entry barrier especially if you don't have money to start investing and you can quickly get the experience and connections (not to mention make some real money). Many real estate gurus enjoy promoting this strategy. But do not be fooled, this isn't a magic bullet. You still need to put in the effort and have the right knowledge. And you need to be good at winning people's trust.

Avoid this mistake: Don't approach this with the "lazy man's mindset." It's not just about finding buyers, it's also about being really good at spotting great deals and motivated sellers who are willing to trust you. Your marketing won't just take care of itself; you've got to be super proactive, and even though anyone can do wholesaling, those who are well equipped with strong marketing funnels are the ones who grow and scale their businesses faster.

If you chose to go with this strategy, be persistent, increase your people skills and wholesaling knowledge, and you will generate a good income stream while you continue to master other more profitable forms of investing.

House hacking

House hacking is a strategy many newbie investors are leveraging when they first enter the real estate arena. It involves purchasing a two, three or four unit property then living in one unit and renting out the others.

Most people will start off with a single-family house when they invest in real estate but smart investors who understand the importance of cash flow follow a different route.

By investing in at least a duplex, you minimize the possibility of becoming a slave to your house expenses such as mortgage, taxes repair and maintenance costs.

The benefit of doing a house hacking strategy is that when done right you could actually live for free. Your property will produce cash flow for you as it continues to appreciate over time.

For example. You could buy a quadplex, live in one of the units and rent out the rest. Since it's still considered a residential unit, you only need to get one loan to cover it, and if you crunch your numbers right and find the right deal, you can end up with a property that pays for all your expenses.

Avoid this mistake: Don't jump into a deal too soon. Take your time and do as much research as possible to find the ideal one for you that produces enough cash flow to cover your costs.

You also need to make sure you vet the tenants thoroughly and implement policies and procedures that protect you and your family in case something goes wrong with the tenants. Most novice real estate investors forget to take these precautionary steps, and it ends up costing them a lot financially and legally.

Live-In-House Flips

This strategy works best for an investor who is very patient, doesn't mind living in a construction zone and also enjoys DIY projects. It is a very hands-on type of real estate investing, but some have enjoyed enormous profits doing it.

Live in house flipping involves purchasing a home that requires a lot of rehabilitation, fixing it while living in it full time and then selling it for a profit.

Avoid this mistake: Don't get into live-in-house flips if you don't understand construction and contractors. Too many people are blindsided by issues like termites or cracks in the foundation, which can only be overcome when one has sufficient knowledge and understanding of how construction works. You also need to have an eye for good property deals so that you can get one that will sell well when the time comes.

Lastly, don't jump into this strategy unless you have a reasonable budget in place, cash reserves and a lot of patience. Sometimes the construction work needed may take longer than expected, or the house may not sell when you want it to sell, and you need to be okay with keeping money tied up until then.

Student rentals

Using this strategy won't be glamorous, but it can be very lucrative. Student rental investing is about providing students a great place to live when they leave home and making a significant income in the process. They often give a robust cash flow. You could buy a house for $300,000 and generate $3,500 per month in rental income because in many cases you could have even seven students living in a house paying $500 per room.

One of the major challenges to this otherwise lucrative strategy is the lease. You need to make sure you keep a single contract in place so that the student house doesn't become a rooming house. Which means although there are many rents to be collected each month, they need to be carried under a single lease and with technology, there are lots of simple processes in place to help with this, but you still need to be hands-on for this strategy to work.

Avoid this mistake: Don't get lured in by the cash flow this strategy generates. Make sure you understand all the financing and legislation aspects required to make this strategy a success. Normally each city has its own legislation, which specifies how to limit these types of housing.

Some cities in housing grant license for students at about $ 450 the first year and then decrease in subsequent years. There's no denying, this strategy is time-consuming and needs a hands-on approach because most of the students will keep calling for assistance so do your due diligence and become aware of all your costs and responsibilities before jumping in.

Buy and Hold

I consider this to be one of the purest forms of real estate investing. It involves purchasing a property, renting it out for an extended period and eventually selling it for profit. If you invest in a buy and hold strategy, the primary objective would be to rent out the purchased property to collect a monthly cash flow and then eventually selling it out in future profitably.

One of the benefits of using this strategy (if you're doing it right) is that the mortgage on the property will pay itself out through the monthly cash flow generated decreasing your principal balance and increasing your equity over time.

Avoid this mistake: Don't buy deals that don't yield a positive cash flow. Learn to evaluate properties thoroughly and avoid making the same mistake made by many new investors make.

Every decision you make including managing your expenses, choosing the right tenant, managing your assets are all crucial to your success. If done poorly they can result in significant loses. But these are all mistakes that can be avoided with the right knowledge.

There is also a real estate marketing cycle that you need to understand and leverage when making your buy-and-hold decisions.

Every market will be different. You need to identify the ebbs and flow of the marketplace where your property is located. Then you need to increase your education, learn to evaluate properties, find good deals and great tenants.

Short Term Rentals

Short-term rentals are very alluring. They are actually considered the fast way of making money in real estate. This is the Airbnb style of real estate investing where you purchase a property and rent it out on a short-term basis. Usually, the rents are very high, and if your property is in a touristic location, you could charge higher rents and expect to be booked out for most of the year.

Because you're here as a beginner in real estate investing, it's important to remind you that location is everything if you're going to go for this strategy.

The main reason Airbnb properties do so well is they serve as a substitute for hotels and motels. There is also a lot of direct contact between the host/owner and the tenants.

Offering a unique and unforgettable experience to your guests is what will help you grow a thriving business with short term rentals so you'll need to either prepare yourself to be more hands-on or hire some professional help.

One more thing you also need to keep in mind is the increased competition from other landlords doing the same, as well as the high turnover of renters who only occupy the place for short durations.

Avoid this mistake: Get clarity on the type of real estate investor you want to be. If long term, consistent passive income is what you're after, and you want optimal results then don't get into short-term rentals expecting such results. This strategy is not for everyone, and usually, the more dynamic investor looking for short-term gain in real estate is the type who will enjoy this strategy.

Get educated on what makes Airbnb properties successful and make sure you're willing to go all in and deliver in both tangible and intangible ways to the clientele that need short term rentals.

Long Term Rentals

In long term rentals passive income is the real deal. It is not as easy as it may sound. It needs patience. Airbnb can be a good example of a long-term rental.

Turnkey Investing

This investment strategy has a longer learning curve and can be scary for some, but if you acquire the right knowledge, the benefits of turnkey investing are fantastic. When you hear real estate gurus talking about passive income and getting real estate to work for you, this is one of those strategies that can help you accomplish all that and more. Passive income is the primary objective of investing in a turnkey property.

This strategy is actually straightforward and can be quite flexible, but the ultimate concept behind turnkey is that you as an investor don't need to be hands-on with the investment. Your role is to "turn the key" on a piece of property and make good money from it. Some investors consider turnkey investing as a property that is already fixed and rented with a third-party company managing it.

In such as a case all that the investor does is make the investment and get paid any profit.

Other investors consider turnkey investing to be a property that might need some rehabilitation. In such a case the investor would need to fix it up a bit, maybe even find tenants to rent but then turn the management over to someone else. At that point, the investor would sit on the sidelines collecting income from the investment without having to deal with the day-to-day operations.

You get to define what "turnkey investing" will mean for you. Regardless of how you define it, there are two components to always bear in mind.

Your opportunities for investing are unlimited

A major benefit of not being limited to local real estate investing is that you can access areas where houses are for sale for less money.

You will be able to buy a property for less, make the property better and then get income from it. And the best part is this strategy allows you to step away from all the work required to own and manage a property (which is usually a full-time job), and just make money. If you do your research well and partner up with the right turnkey real estate company, they might even buy the house first, clean it up and then sell it to you. They make their money by managing it, and you own the property.

Avoid this mistake: Try not to buy a property without seeing it or knowing its real potential. Understandably, the fact that the property could be a long distance away from you might make it hard for you to personally vet the property. But I still argue against it. Some real estate investors do this, and it's such a gamble. It could work out well, or it could end up being a lemon that costs more money than it makes.

There are always risks involved with any real estate investing but blindly jumping into a deal merely because it's a turnkey investment opportunity is a grievous mistake that's unnecessary. Smart real estate investors do everything possible to gain as much first-hand knowledge of the property before making an investment. I recommend you always do the same even with this strategy.

All the strategies we've shared work. The one best suited for you depends entirely on your objectives, personality and your "WHY."

The business plan we created in an earlier chapter will guide you into choosing the right strategy because you'll see which one aligns perfectly with that road map that you created for yourself. This is a decision you need to make for yourself based on how much effort you want to put into growing your real estate business. Now that you're well on your way to your first deal let's get into the mathematics and financing so we can ensure this activity leads you to financial freedom.

Chapter 7. Managing a full-time job and Real Estate

More and more people with no prior real estate experience are quitting their jobs and going in full time to build their fortunes because as you might have guessed, it's not being viewed as one of the best ways to gain financial freedom. But not everyone should just quit their job. Sometimes, it's not even the right thing to do.

If you were wondering whether it is possible to keep your job and still grow a real estate business, then this chapter is for you. You can absolutely keep working a day job while expanding your portfolio.

In fact, one of the benefits of keeping your job and becoming a real estate investor is that you don't become dependent on it at the start. The cash flow generated by your new investments can go into exponentially growing your portfolio while you live off the salary from your day job. This can quickly fast track your business.

Having a stable income also helps with financing because banks will be more willing to help you out when you've got a credible 9-to-5. So if you already have a day job, don't just quit, there's much good that can come from it and you can already begin growing your portfolio by investing in a buy-and-hold deal with property management, partnering in a larger piece of property, investing in mortgages (notes) or serving as a private money lender.

There really is no right or wrong way to approach real estate as long as you have clarity on how much effort you're willing to put in. Whether you do it full time or part time you can still work your way into financial freedom. The most important thing is that you do a self-check and follow your gut when it comes to starting this.

If you're unemployed, the choice is plain and clear, but if you currently have a job, please don't just quit because you hear people on YouTube advertising how they quit their jobs and made millions.

You need to follow your own path and make informed decisions if you want this business to succeed.

That said, it's important also to emphasize that you can be able to figure this out on your own regardless of whether you do it full time or part-time. Real estate investing is not rocket science, and there are countless stories of average individuals who have self-taught themselves into vast fortunes.

A common question many new investors will ask is:

Do I need a guru to be rich?

The simple and short answer is absolutely not! You don't need a guru for anything really because you are the determining factor in your life.

Whether it's a health, relationship or financial goal, only you can make it happen. Oftentimes gurus are just external motivators.

However, I do recommend getting some kind of mentor. A mentor does not need to be a guru, and quite frankly I hope you get a mentor that isn't a guru because at least they will genuinely make time for you and help you walk this path of real estate investing without the hyperbole of fancy cars, models and getting rich quick.

It is, in fact, true that there's a real estate guru trap you need to avoid, but that doesn't mean you shut out all experts. Some individuals are very knowledgeable and genuine, but you must do your homework and refuse to get caught up in the hype, empty promises, and wishful thinking.

How do you deal with expensive markets when starting out with no money?

It's tough to start out in an expensive marketplace if you've got no cash in hand. There's no easy way around this. The best thing you can do is to get creative and innovative. Utilize the resources at hand, amplify your skills and use all the tricks, strategies and options I have detailed in this book. Without persistence, perseverance and lots of creativity, you just won't go very far regardless of the marketplace you're in.

I have shared several strategies of how you can start small, how to find private money lenders or partner up with someone who has what you're lacking and you've read numerous stories of people who've been able to succeed even when the cards were stacked against them.

If your market is tough to crack and you really don't have the cash, consider the Turnkey investing option we talked about. But even then, do your due diligence and make sure it's right for you.

Before we move on, there's one more thing worth talking about that most skip over.

When should you get a LLC and how do you start?

Many novice real estate investors are usually confused about getting an LLC, so it's only fair we touch on it here. And then you can make an informed decision over when you'll need one.

Not every real estate investor needs an LLC especially those just starting out, but of course, as your business grows it is advisable to get one.

A limited liability company is meant to protect you from potential lawsuits related to the property.

Nevertheless, the trouble of forming and maintaining a company may not be worthwhile protection anyway, especially if you breach some of the clauses (which will often happen for self-starters and small business owners who often co-mingle personal and business funds). There are other affordable options if you're just starting out that could protect you from the theoretical threat of a lawsuit.

To get started on your limited liability company I recommend following these five simple steps:

Step 1: Choose Your State

As a new real estate investor, the best option is to form your limited liability company in the state where you live and where you plan to conduct your business. If you plan on capitalizing in properties in different states, then you'll must register for a foreign LLC in every state where you'll do business. You should know however that although business-friendly states like Nevada are great for registering your LLC, there's a lot of paperwork and extra fees involved.

Step 2: Choose a name for your LLC

Every state has its own rubrics about the kind of names an LLC can have. Do a name search online and learn about the laws in your state and pick a suitable name. Here are a few guidelines to help you get started.

- Your name must contain the phrase "limited liability company" or (LLC or L.L.C)
- You may be required by some Banks or Attorneys to provide additional paperwork and have a licensed individual (doctor, lawyer, etc.) as part of your LLC.
- The name you choose should not contain words that could confuse your LLC with a government organization (State Department, FBI, Treasury, etc.).

Step 3: Select a registered Agent

The next thing you need is to assign a registered agent (either a person or a business) that will send and received legal papers on your behalf. Official correspondence documents such as legal summons and registered filings will be received by your registered agent and forwarded to you.

Most states need every LLC to recommend a registered agent. This agent must be a resident of the state you're doing business in, or a corporation authorized to conduct business in that state.

Step 4: File your LLC with The State

The fourth step you must take is to file your documents with the state. This is basically how you create an LLC. This document is usually referred to as "Articles of Organization" or "Certificate of Formation" or "Certificate of Organization.

Your LLC document is destined to outline the organizational structure of your business. You'll also need to decide between appointing a manager for your LLC or have it be co-managed by the owners.

Step 5: Create an LLC Operating Agreement

The last step before you're ready to make your first purchase under your new LLC is to create an operating agreement. This is a legal document that outlines the ownership configuration and member roles of your new LLC.

The good news is that most states in America don't have this as a requirement, but I still encourage you to create it anyways. Check in with your state to find out if it's mandatory. There are six main segments of an operating agreement.

Organization - indicates when and where the company was formed, who the members are and how the property is defined.

Voting and Management - addressing how the company is managed as well as how the members vote.

Capital Aids - casing which members financially support the LLC, and how more funds will be raised in the future.

Distributions - Delineating how the company's profits and losses are shared among members.

Membership Changes - Describing the process for adding or removing members, as well as when members can transfer their ownership shares.

Dissolution - Explains the conditions in which the LLC may be dissolved.

After following these steps carefully, you'll now be the owner of your very own LLC. After which you're ready to start growing your real estate business with more ease and peace of mind.

I do recommend also obtaining an Employer Identification Number (EIN) once you've formed the LLC. It is the same as social security number for your LLC.

And remember, you must separate your personal assets from your business, register your LLC for state taxes, set up accounting, and get yourself more protection with business insurance especially if you're going to be a landlord.

With all this knowledge in place, it's time to give you a simple process to help you go from ideation to your first purchase. As a beginner, if you do these four things diligently, you will close your first deal successfully.

Chapter 8. The 4 steps to Real Estate success

The only secret sauce that will enable you to start winning with real estate from your very first deal.

1) Find the deal

The first thing you need to do is find an incredible deal on a property that you love. If you don't love the property, don't invest in it. And the trick here is to find a deal that you love because the property resonates with you and the numbers are also good. You can't afford to compromise on either of this if you want to hit a home run.

How do I find the deal? Well, I have shared so many tactics and ideas on where to start looking for deals in this book. Check in your local paper, visit trusted websites like Zillow go on MLS sites or call up real estate agents in the area you want to do business. If you are going to flip houses or do wholesaling, paid ads are also a great channel and when leveraged properly social media can bring you lots of leads with just a tiny budget.

Make sure you have your criterion clearly outlined when you start finding your deals.

Read through all the ideas contained in this book several times, test them out, drive for dollars if you have to, build relationships with real estate agents so they can keep you in the loop on hot deals.

Get creative and leverage social media and paid advertising if your budget allows. Whatever you need to do to always have a full pipeline of potential deals - do it!

Real world example:

Let's assume you live in Philadelphia and you've landed on an incredible 4-unit deal. This feels like the right fit for you. You have enough knowledge, and you've decided it's time to take the leap of faith and invest in your first property. The property is a 3,656 sqft that goes for $260,000, and since you're doing it as a private residential purchase, you can expect a down payment of 5%. Now it's time to talk about where you can get the money.

2) Financing the deal

Most people think this is the biggest obstacle to closing that first deal, but in truth, it isn't. If you have an incredible deal finding the resources to make it happen won't be impossible. You can go to any American Bank to finance your deal.

You can use one of the many alternatives I shared in the chapter on finance, and if you are going to live in one of the units (I highly recommend this strategy when getting started) then you can get an FHA (see glossary) so you can get the best loan with the lowest down payment.

How do I finance the 4-unit property that costs $260,000?

By living in one of the units, you could easily go to FHA and put 5% down which amounts to $13,000.

Essentially, you'll be the owner of a property that's worth a quarter of a million dollars, yet you only invested $13,000 and if you can do the next steps right and hold on to this property long enough, in 30 years the property will be debt free, and it will have appreciated in value.

3) Analyzing the deal

This is where you get to test and see if the 4-unit property makes sense to invest in. You must do a preliminary title search to ensure the property is good to invest and also to ensure it's worth the investment.

The most important thing when analyzing your first deal is to figure out whether the property is profitable in terms of cash flow.

You also need to know if the numbers make sense in relation to cap rate; the internal rate of return and you must work out the cash flow before and after taxes.

The mathematics doesn't need to be complicated or overwhelming. Keep it as basic as possible, use the formula outlined in the chapter on financing as well as the formulas I shared within the glossary.

There are also many resources online like Biggerpockets.com that offer online calculators to help you analyze deals quickly.

Getting back to our 4-unit property, here are some basic calculations that would apply here.

Property = $260,000

5% down payment = $13,000 which means you need to finance $247,000. The debt that you'll need to pay annually can be rounded off to $15000.

Annual income from this will be $34,200.

The expense of maintaining this can be assumed to be 50% of your income as a fair approximation, but since you're managing the property and fixing it, the cost should be lower.

So, let's assume this will cost you $12,000 annually.

That leaves you with $22,200 - $15,000 = $7,200 positive cash flow which is about 50% ROI on your original down payment.

Not too shabby for your first deal.

This is a fundamental example of how you must analyze your deals.

4) Managing the deal

Assuming you're going to fix and maintain this first deal, the cost of repairing and running the place should be kept minimal, so it doesn't eat up on your profits.

How do I manage the deal? To get the numbers I just shared above using that FHA loan, you need to fix and manage that property yourself. You also need to live in it for the first year. And you must continue paying yourself rent as well if you're a savvy investor. If you do your job right as a property manager, you could comfortably raise the rent on the property. Even as little as $50 per month annually, you'll be amazed how fast your income can grow over time. By now I am sure you can see that you don't need hundreds of thousands to start your real estate journey.

Chapter 9. Buying and Closing on a Property

Now that you know the steps it takes to purchase a home; you are going to have to look deeper at the expenses and the other important information that some investors overlook when they first start out. You can see the asking price of a house simply for what it is, but that is only the main portion of what you're actually going to have to pay.

Once you have decided which property to purchase, it can be an exciting time. The thrill of the sale and knowing that you are investing in your future. All that anxiety over the purchase hasn't ended just yet as you still have to go through an inspection.

Closing can be just as stressful as the buying process for many investors and homeowners in general. Before closing, there is always a chance that the deal will still fall through. Remember that when investing.

Financing and Loans

You might be an investor going into this brand-new, all on your own. Perhaps you know other investors that got you interested in the market. Whatever it is, you likely already have a method of financing that you are preparing. Perhaps it is a loan with others, or maybe you are financing it all on your own.

If you aren't sure what you want to do, there are still plenty of options for you. Cash financing is usually the easiest option because it is your own money that you don't have to worry about paying back. You can use a private money lender who is a knowledgeable investor looking for prospects like you to get started.

You could even have the option of seller financing, in which you and the seller strike up a deal. When you choose to do this, it is important to ensure that you are still getting the legal protection needed should something go wrong.

Mortgages

Mortgages are amounts borrowed used to purchase real estate in which the buyer is promised to pay back within a certain time frame with the real estate being collateral for the payment. Most mortgages are taken out through banks. If the mortgage payments are consistently missed and all other options were exhausted by the owner, then the bank can foreclose on a home, meaning that they are then the owners.

Mortgages are how people are able to afford houses because rarely can someone afford to buy a house outright. A person with a job that pays $50,000 a year would have to wait a decade to buy a $200,000 house, but with a mortgage, they just might be able to pay for it.

This is the avenue that people will most often take when purchasing a home, and it is something for you to consider. Your payments will be based on your income, credit score, and the amount of the house. The more expensive the house, the higher the mortgage. The worse your credit score, the higher your interest rates.

Fixed vs. Adjustable

A fixed loan is one in which the interest rate will not change as time goes on. This means if you start with a 10 percent APR, it stays that way even if the economy crashes or does astronomically better. Your interest rate will never change with a fixed loan.

When it is adjustable, it can be altered depending on time and a few other factors that might increase or decrease the interest amount. This means you might pay 1 percent interest in the first six months, then 5 percent in the next six, 10 percent after the first year, and a 3 percent increase each year until a maximum percentage is reached.

Adjustable rates will usually be initially lower than the rates of a fixed interest. You will often be able to know the interest rate that will be there in the future, but sometimes there might be a determining factor that raises it.

You should determine what's best for you based on the time that you will be owning that home. For example, if you're only going to be owning for three months, an adjustable loan with an interest rate of 5 percent would be better than a fixed loan at 5 percent. A fixed loan is usually better for those that are planning on holding on to their property for a while.

Real Estate Mortgage Broker

A mortgage broker is a way that you can find good options for financing your home. These people are experts in mortgages and know how to find the right one based on your needs.

You might pay for the broker, but they're often paid for by the lenders. This helps you have a useful resource that will ensure you're making the right investment and not one blindly based on the first thing that seemed to work.

This is going to be especially helpful depending on what kind of loan you are deciding to take, fixed or adjustable. A mortgage broker will find you deals that will work best for you and give you comparable rates so you can feel confident you're making the best choice.

Down Payment

It is a good rule of thumb to have at least 20 percent of a down payment for the investment property of your choice. Some people will say 15 percent, but in terms of investing, you always want more.

The more that you put down, the lower your interest rates will be. The lower your mortgages might be as well, which could be helpful if you're investing long-term.

More financial standards need to be considered when saving money for your investment property. You want to have the money for the down payment, but there will be a lot of other hidden costs as well. You can expect that there will be fees, taxes, and insurance rates close to 3–10 percent of the market value on a home.

Your credit score and current financial standing could also affect what your payments might be. This is why it's important to make sure that you're not just someone with money but a person in a decent financial standing to make sure you can avoid paying unnecessarily high fees.

Types of Costs

First, you have to think of the cost of a house, and then you have to look at what you are going to be getting back. When you see that amount, you have to know it is actually going to end up being less than that because of all the costs that go into a home.

Of course, if you are renovating the homes, there will be a much higher cost. Even when you're considering renovations, don't forget other hidden fees beyond basic construction and furnishing. You might need to pay for more inspectors, and perhaps you have to get something re-zoned or pay a higher tax fee.

If you won't be renovating, there's still fees and other types of finances that you have to consider. We'll go over some of them in the next few sections, but remember that these aren't all the fees that you'll be experiencing.

Property Tax

Property taxes are yearly fees that we have to pay based on our home's value and location. Value is determined by the home's size, age, and renovations. Adding a room might increase the value of a home. At the same time, demolishing an old building could also increase property value. Location is simply where your property is. A lot close to the beach in California is going to have higher taxes than a lot of the same size in middle-of-nowhere Iowa.

Make sure you look into how exactly your property taxes will be calculated but understand that there are very few similar things all investments will qualify for. Your property taxes are going to be calculated by not only the land but also the buildings that are on that land as well.

Inspection Fees

Inspections are necessary in order for a house to close. When the house is in escrow, this is when inspectors are usually called to come and look at the house. They will check for structure, infestation, and anything in the building that is not up to code. This is why it can be helpful if you have an inspector on your team when looking at homes, though they can't conduct official inspections until the house is in escrow.

You have to make sure that you are prepared to pay for this inspection. They are typically around $200–$400, depending on the location and size of the home. The inspectors are paid by the buyers. If you're making a very large investment over six digits, you might want to consider more than one inspector to make sure nothing is overlooked. Running into unexpected costs during renovation can be what really sets you back and puts you over budget.

Aside from the inspection fees, be prepared to pay for anything that might need to be fixed in the inspection. Perhaps a beam needs to be relocated or a pool needs filled in. You might work this into your deal with the seller as well should there be anything especially financially heavy.

Loan Costs

In addition to having to pay back the money that you are borrowing for a certain investment, you'll also be responsible for paying any fees and interest acquired throughout as well.

Loan costs will be less the less you borrow, and the better your credit history is. You also have to consider closing costs on whatever your borrowed agreement is.

This includes any fees for acquiring documents, such as the application or your credit history. There will be insurance premiums, various inspections, taxes, and many other hidden fees that you can't overlook. You should be prepared to pay anywhere from 2 percent to 6 percent of the initial purchase price when it comes to closing costs.

Insurance Title

Since you are making an investment, there is going to be some risk involved. You'll have to make sure that you are prepared to pay title insurance to protect the lender. This is a way to secure their faith in you and protect them from losses acquired.

Though it protects the lender, you'll still be responsible for purchasing it. They might also require that you purchase an owner's insurance for yourself.

Negotiating Skills

There are a lot of different costs and fees, so it will be up to you to negotiate your best prices. While some people will have fixed prices, there will be a lot of negotiation involved in this kind of investing. The better you are at looking for good deals and convincing others to buy into these, the more money you will make in the end.

Don't say yes the first time. Let your investments get out there a little bit. If you say yes right away, it gives the buyer the idea that they could have bid lower and vice versa.

Be a cooperative person. No one will like to invest with you if it is difficult. The more you can network and build meaningful relationships in this business, the better off you will be in the long run.

Stand up for what you think is right. It will let people know that you are not going to settle for anything less than what you know you deserve.

Chapter 10. While Owning

Once you finish the deal and get to a point where you are now a property owner, the work doesn't stop. Now, instead of a prospective buyer, you are on the other end as a property owner.

Don't wait around to get started with your next step as an owner. It can be very easy to get lost in projects. Keep up that same drive that led you to the purchase in the first place so you can stay on track with your goals and get your property sold ASAP.

If you are going to be holding on to the property for longer, then it is going to be important that you know what it means to be a landlord or lessor to the people that will be renting your home.

Upkeep

If you are keeping up a rented property, then upkeep is going to be very important. This is going to include all the maintenance involved in making sure that a property doesn't depreciate. You can do this yourself, or you can hire a team responsible for maintenance.

If you want to own a rental property for the next few decades, you have to be ready for larger costs like reroofing, replacing appliances, fixing the plumbing. There will be some long-term costs that can be covered by monthly rent of tenants, but there might be some things you just have to do out of pocket.

Remember that other people will be responsible for some upkeep, like keeping the floors clean and the garbage picked up, and that might not even happen. If renting to people with pets, that can cause property destruction as well. Though you will want to cover this before they move in through move-in fees or deposits, it can still be costly and time-consuming to fix up the damage other renters might have done.

Doing Inspections

Though you did some initial inspections to determine property value and to see whether the house was in good shape, you'd still have to do them as a homeowner. If you want to do inspections while someone else is living there, then it is going to be up to you to make sure that is written and agreed upon, as renters have their rights as well.

If you are going to be investing in vacation, then you might consider having an inspection or cleaning fee to make sure that people will keep the place in good shape.

Adding Value to Property

It can be expensive to upgrade a home, but if you let it sit and make no changes, that can have just as much of a negative dent on your finances.

Adding value can simply be different cosmetic things. You might want to knock down a wall in a home or paint the outside a different color. Though you can get big returns from doing gut rehabs, you can also find your money working for itself when you make a few simple changes that increase the desire for a certain property.

Avoid getting too personal with the touches that you add. You want to look at every decision as one for the future of the home, not just based on the things that you already enjoy.

Rolling over Rental Property Profits

You might get to a point in your rental journey where you decide that you want to roll over your rental property profits into another real estate investment. The IRS identifies any attempt as an investment as such.

To do this, you might want to use a 1031 tax-free exchange, which will help when filling out your yearly returns. This is also known as a Starker Trust. It will help so you can defer these taxes rather than have to pay on the capital gains made during the initial investment.

REITs

REIT stands for real estate investment trusts. A REIT is a company in which ownership is obtained over real estate that is producing income. There are different requirements that a company has to meet in order to be considered a REIT.

These companies are beneficial to real estate investments because they give all investors the chance to make real money from their purchases. A REIT company will help provide competitive returns based on dividend income as well as capital appreciation.

Selling Real Estate

Once you've gone through all the steps of initially hunting, buying, and closing, it is time now to move on to the part where you make a sale that leads to a return.

The best way to make a good sale is to use a real estate agent as they will help to get you the highest price since they will get a high return as well.

Ensure that you are making the most from your home. If you are investing in multiple places at a time, it will be easier for you to decide longer term when to sell and if you should stay invested.

Conclusion.

It will be hard at first. Eventually, however, you will find that you can actually gain financial independence from real estate investing. If you decide to flip houses and buy and sell rapidly, then you will see that each sale you make gets bigger and bigger. On the other hand, you can also decide to keep properties and add more, only increasing how much money you are making monthly.

Each time you reach a goal, look at it as the starting point for a new one. Reach further to fund your future. Look for innovative ways that you can grow your investments. No matter how much money you're making, remember you can always make more.

While it is important to secure yourself for the future, make sure that you are still allowing this increase in wealth as a chance to take some risks. You won't want to be too risky in the beginning, but as time goes on, you will find it's easier to make more challenging decisions.

Attaining financial security through investments in realty is more than just a plan to fantasize about during your lunch break at your 9 to 5 job. Turning this dream into a reality prepares you for an early retirement.

In order to do this, cleanse yourself and your thoughts from the common notions of wealth and money. Should you insist on following what you were told is the standard route to wealth, then you are fast approaching a dead end.

Financial security is nothing about being confined in a cycle of slaving for money, piling it up, and praying that one day this money delivers protection. You've been led to believe that piling your hard-earned money in a 401k, IRA, stocks, or annuities will someday grant you that privilege to live a hedonistic life and bother no more about your finances. Recent records have proven that this doesn't work. Investments in realty is a different story, however.

In order to attain financial security, think first about investing in real estate. Are you still asking what makes investing in real estate the correct path towards attaining a fortune? This should answer your question. For beginners, you can start with little risk and little or no cash while sticking to your full-time job.

Second, rental realty provides you with a flow of passive income every month which eases you slowly from the clutches of that stress-filled 9 to 5 job.

Third, it's easy to control the equity in your properties to purchase more rental units or to finance other businesses that provide an automatic and a lasting source of income.

58600364R00056

Made in the USA
Middletown, DE
07 August 2019